# Crow-Blue, Crow-Black

# CROW-BLUE, CROW-BLACK

CHIP LIVINGSTON

The New York Quarterly Foundation, Inc.
New York, New York

NYQ Books™ is an imprint of The New York Quarterly Foundation, Inc.

The New York Quarterly Foundation, Inc.
P. O. Box 2015
Old Chelsea Station
New York, NY 10113

www.nyqbooks.org

Copyright © 2012 by Chip Livingston

All rights reserved. No part of this book may be used or reproduced in any manner whatsoever without written permission of the author except in the case of brief quotations embodied in critical articles and reviews.

First Edition

Set in New Baskerville

Layout and Design by Raymond P. Hammond

Cover Illustration: "Duality", 11" x 14" oil on canvas
 ©2009 Deb Kirkeeide | www.debkirkeeide.com

Author photo: ©2012 Gabriel Padilha | www.gabrielpadilha.com

Library of Congress Control Number: 2012933644

ISBN: 978-1-935520-57-3

# Crow-Blue, Crow-Black

## *Acknowledgments*

Eternal thanks to the Creator and All the Helpers. This book wouldn't be possible without the guidance and friendship of the poet Ai; teachers Lou Asekoff, Sapphire, Lisa Jarnot, Linda Hogan, and Lucia Berlin; Spanish language teachers at La Herradura in Montevideo, Uruguay; poets Joy Harjo, Brad Gooch, Kenward Elmslie, Aaron Smith, James Thomas Stevens, and Allison Adelle Hedge Coke; first readers Suzanne Kingsbury, Lauren Myers, and Cecilia Johnson; family in Florida, Alabama, Kentucky, Colorado, and Rhode Island; extended family in Argentina; the Poarch Band of Muskogee Creek Indians; writing programs at Brooklyn College, University of Colorado, and Gotham Writers Workshops; NYQ Books; Soul Mountain Retreat; Victoria Bond, Barbara Parry, Gabriel Insiburo, and Gabriel Padilha; the loving memory of Ash and Kimberley Jordan; and the editors of the following journals where the following poems were first published:

*ALARUM* (a chapbook from Other Rooms Press): ST. FRANCIS IS A VERB;
*Argestes*: SNAKEBIRD;
*Art & Understanding*: POEM TO MY BOYFRIEND'S HIV;
*Barrow Street*: THE TITLE OF THE PAINTING IS ST. THOMAS;
*Blue Stem Quarterly*: CARDINAL CROSS;
*Cincinnati Review*: TRUMPET;
*Columbia Poetry Review*: OCTOBER CITY;
*Court Green*: FOR TIM (WHO SAYS HI TO DAVID), GOOGLISM FOR: JOE BRAINARD, CELEBRITIES ON GREENWICH AVENUE, WHO'S PRETENDING?, MARS CONJUNCT VENUS;
*Drunken Boat*: L-M-N-ATION;
*Eleven Eleven*: JOHN WAYNE'S OLD PORNOS;
*Florida Review*: MIXED-BLOOD AT CATHOLIC SCHOOL, COME TO THE DEN OF MY HILLS, A PROPOSAL;
*Front Porch*: ST. NICHOLAS;

*Georgetown Review*: SHEDDING;
*Hinchas de Poesia*: MISIONES, BITING ON GINGER;
*Lilies & Cannonballs Review*: HOLIDAYS IN ABU GHRAIB;
*MiPOesias*: ST. SOLOMON & THE REPTILES;
*Mudfish*: GREENWICH AVENUE;
*New American Writing*: GOOD DOG;
*New York Quarterly*: MERCURY IN URANUS, IF *NANCY* WAS AARON SMITH, FINDING LOVE IN CHELSEA, DAD JOKES AROUND BEFORE DEFINING AIDS;
*Pearl*: EVOLUTION;
*Potomac Review*: HOW IS IT?;
*The Queen City Review*: INSPIDERED;
*Poui*: EXTERIORS;
*Skidrow Penthouse*: WHO'S PRETENDING?;
*SING: POETRY OF THE INDIGENOUS AMERICAS* (U. of Arizona Press): CROW-BLUE, CROW-BLACK; SEPTIPUS; PUNTA DEL ESTE PANTOUM; HOW IS IT?;
*Solstice*: IEMANJA, POSTCARDS FOR KENWARD;
*SOVEREIGN EROTICS* (U. of Arizona Press): MAN COUNTRY;
*Subtropics*: Poem$^X$;
*Talking Stick*: TO REMOVE ANGER, TO SING A MAN'S LOVE TO YOU;
*Yellow Medicine Review*: HUNTING SON.

DEDICATED TO GABRIEL PADILHA

# Contents

## CROW-BLUE: *south turns north*

POEM<sup>x</sup> (THAT I THOUGHT BROKE MY HEART) / 15
CORVUS & HYDRA / 16
TO REMOVE ANGER / 17
ST. FRANCIS IS A VERB / 18
POEM TO MY BOYFRIEND'S HUMAN IMMUNODEFICIENCY VIRUS / 19
SHEDDING / 21
OCTOBER CITY / 22
GREENWICH AVENUE / 23
JOHN WAYNE'S OLD PORNOS / 24
EVOLUTION / 25
COME TO THE DEN OF MY HILLS / 27
YELLOW / 28
QUANTUM LEAP / 29
MISTAKEN IDENTITY / 30
CELEBRITIES ON GREENWICH AVENUE / 31
L-M-N-ATION / 33
CARDINAL CROSS / 34
ON THE WAY TO BROTHERHOOD / 35
23 / 36
DAD JOKES AROUND BEFORE DEFINING AIDS / 37
VENUS RETROGRADE / 38
HOLIDAYS IN ABU GHRAIB / 39
MERCURY IN URANUS / 40
NORTHEAST KINGDOM / 41
YESTERDAY. TOILET. FLUSH. / 42
IF *NANCY* WAS AARON SMITH / 44
FOR THE DOUBTS / 45
FOR TIM (*WHO SAYS HI TO DAVID*) / 47
GOOGLISM FOR: JOE BRAINARD / 48


CROW-BLUE, CROW-BLACK / 51

## CROW-BLACK: *north turns south*

THIRTEEN CROW FEATHERS / *55*
HOW IS IT? / *56*
MIXED-BLOOD AT CATHOLIC SCHOOL / *57*
TO SING A MAN'S LOVE TO YOU / *58*
MEDIODÍA / *59*
SPIDER MEDICINE / *60*
HUNTING SON / *61*
EXTERIORS / *62*
WHO'S PRETENDING? / *63*
A JOYFUL NOISE / *64*
THE TITLE OF THE PAINTING IS SAINT THOMAS / *65*
PUNTA DEL ESTE PANTOUM / *66*
ST. NICHOLAS / *67*
ANÓ GRANDE (YOU COPYRIGHTED YOUR NAME AND NOW I HAVE TO PAY YOU TO SAY IT) / *68*
GOOD DOG / *69*
TRUMPET / *70*
MARS CONJUNCT VENUS / *71*
BITING ON GINGER / *72*
ST. SOLOMON AND THE REPTILES / *73*
MISIONES / *74*
POSTCARDS FOR KENWARD / *75*
SEPTIPUS / *77*
MAN COUNTRY / *78*
SNAKEBIRD / *79*
"WE OURSELVES SEE IN ALL RIVERS" / *80*
INSPIDERED / *81*
IEMANJA / *82*
MIRROR SONNET / *83*
A PROPOSAL / *85*


END NOTES / *87*

# Crow-Blue
*south turns north*

# Poem$^X$ (That I Thought Broke My Heart)

Tell the Mississippi I'm a drunk vigilante
and there are more than x ways to skin a cat,
more than one Godot, more than radical
departure from someone else's last concerto;
there is corpus luteum in prenatal mouse ovaries,
for instance; there's my jumpy sister all legs,
but that's a cockroach in a different pissing contest,
and I'm behaving this way for a couple of reasons,
no longer manipulating the lower case x,
not tag editing the game to a stranger's equation
where $x < (y\,x\,y\,x\,y)$.
I was actually thinking of going Catholic
until the saint switched his appetite, went cable,
got oiled like a ladies man in follicle merriment.
And this is the first reason I have taken the compass,
followed the drinking gourd, why I have given up
the tendency for false false sorrow. The second
started in water, in Apalachee brotherhood,
where x was big, bloated, obsolete—a con
out of prison, and with minutes to the masquerade.
Ignorance was pollinated by small country wings.
You were tail paint, a dead tongue witnessed
and reliably unhinged; but I found a grackle of truth
in my Etruscan slumber and your sleep woke me hoarse.
I'd found something that I couldn't tell the night.
There is fly breath, there is magic, there is beautiful.
There is the x inverted, the x imaginary,
and the x as a negative number.

## Corvus & Hydra

eternally thirsty raven
you were mercury white
like light on water

now you're testing
your reflection
are you vested crow?

a black cuckoo?
the greater fool
for lying to Apollo?

the cup is just
out of your reach
he robbed your speech

but those figs
they made you
    ravenous

## To Remove Anger

That man of black wood, that man with the blankets, give him a place to rest his thundering headspin. Let him see an all-red man removing the venom from the spider. Remaking tobacco with his right hand. To pacify the coiled serpent.

That man of black wood, that man with the blankets, wrap him a stick of red cedar and build him a fire to heat the rocks he carries. Offer those stones creek water and watch them crack into jewels. Help him dig a cave under the wet roots of a cypress tree. Help him bury them.

That man of black wood, that man with the blankets, make him a supper of sofkee and sweetcorn, roast him the red fish you call from the river, feed him ripe scuppernongs picked with your fingers.

That man of black wood, that man with the blankets, remind him he is a kinsman, a red man, a great wizard united with another great wizard, to fail in nothing. Remake tobacco with the left hand in a counterclockwise direction.

## St. Francis is a Verb

Fully loaded with the blessed technology
and just over three hours to complete the diagnosis,
the St. Francis comprises almost two-hundred procedures,
buried is just one of the ways we do that,
the six o'clock split is another unforgettable stop,
and we're just a few of the participants
in your cadaver organ retrieval, just young friars
in saints' forms, dedicating the beacon
at the western end of the powhite parkway.
Indulgence is a vast tomb, one summed up
in your Good Friday letter, gold folded and wishing
the sky, wishing water's scorching flow,
the envied sculptor's thought, Lucifer's single
deep cleft, and thunderbolts shot by hazardous gods,
murdering the throbbing disclosure, exciting
perception independently—a woman growing cloudy
on her feet, and the mirror act of oil,
keeping only the blood-drawn dream,
the confession of St. Francis, certain dealings
secret to minister; his evidence the compass silent
and a solemn promise of anguish.  Surrender
your spiritual narrative, surrender your altar
beads, romantic redemption, dumb glee.
St. Francis tamed the wolf, but the place
of worship is rated NO, and there's no recovery
in the nurse's hut.  The secretary torches
friars' rules, says:   *For dimensions of Jesus,
you must sacrifice sainthood.*

## Poem to My Boyfriend's Human Immuno-deficiency Virus

you are not related to the bowerbird
nor crow nor any bird noted for magnificent plumage
you are not paradisaea apoda, not paradise minor
the king you are not
you are not a place where you can hear live jazz
seven days a week
you are not an island native

you are a shy bloomer
with neither petal nor sepal
not tough, not easily grown
not tolerant of his soil

you are not a family resort
dedicated to making a truly pleasurable vacation
not prized for dramatic display
you are not a charming villa
located on the hillside of bordeaux
you are not a small bird very near the beach

you are not a must
you are not fast growing
you are not a boat

you are forgotten, sterile
not licensed or insured
to cater our parties
you are not more of a bush not even a seed
you are not wild and free
you are not the cinematic equivalent
of one of those island falls

you are closed until further notice
you are not poised to soar
to heights in joyful praise
you are not driving ma crazy
not the scene for the morning breakfast buffet
you are not easily seen from a treetop
you are not reliably evergreen

## SHEDDING

under the porch stone:  a snakeskin
me in the bathtub:  scrubbing off mine
on the red carpet:  Rilke and Satie
in Calais, Vermont:  Helvetia's green door
and every day more Spanish from the tongue
of the oak:  its fall leaves
the cherry trees' spring seeds
clipped nails and eyelashes relinquishing
the pull of yesterday: tomorrow
and today's lukewarm water
pasting pollen to the cypress tree
the stripped bark to the cedar blossom

## October City

immobile was her discontent
her believed other    her doctor's cold fist

105 and Pulitzer pronounced
incorrectly    talk done told herself

the accident remembered    the regained
life spent French    talents created

painting themselves in
delicate fat paint    maybe tribute

maybe myth    the reunited feelings
during which the rumors worried

the customs    unsure suicide attempt
funeral people filled out with troubles

the artist's thoughts internal
before chaser    before flourish

# GREENWICH AVENUE

I'm looking through Tim Dlugos's bedroom
     his diaries     his ashes
He willywhistles in my ear to whisper
     *This is really happening*
Then do me a favor, I say     Say hi to Ash
     say hi to Joe
He catches a laugh in his throat     says
     *Say hi to Kenward*     *no, say hello*

## John Wayne's Old Pornos

I'm looking at John Wayne's old porno tapes
Man that big ass was hairy     spreading his cheeks
& showing teeth     I can't tell if he's gritting
them or smiling     His lasso's looped around
a fellow's neck     choking at a caught spur
or burr in the saddle     I'm looking at
his sideburned blond shadow's suede vest
western stars, boots, and matching Stetson
I'm not looking down a canyon at the antelope or bison
I'm looking at John Wayne with his pants down

# EVOLUTION

*(after Tim Dlugos)*

Anne Hathaway is becoming Audrey Hepburn.
Ed Harris is becoming Harvey Keitel.
Harvey Keitel is becoming Dennis Hopper.
Dennis Hopper, after briefly becoming Charles Bukowski, is becoming Robert De Niro, but unfortunately the De Niro that De Niro became, of *Meet the Fockers* and *Analyze That*, and not the De Niro of *Taxi Driver* (or even *Cape Fear*) that De Niro was.
Liv Tyler is becoming Liz Taylor.
Delta Burke, who thought *she* would become Liz Taylor, is becoming Rip Taylor, and Elizabeth Taylor is becoming Delta Burke.
Gary Coleman is becoming Danny Bonaduce, and vice versa. (*What you talking about, Ricky Schroder?*)
Katie Holmes is becoming Lisa Marie Presley, but at a slightly slower pace than Tom Cruise is becoming Michael Jackson.
Nicole Kidman tried to become Jessica Lange but is becoming Joan Rivers.
Lindsay Lohan is becoming Britney Spears.
Britney Spears is becoming Paula Abdul.
Amy Winehouse is becoming Janice Joplin, who was whom Courtney Love was hoping to become, but Courtney Love became David Lee Roth.
David Lee Roth became a real estate agent, which is similar to but not exactly the same thing as Erik Estrada becoming a spokesman for California recreational properties and the California Highway Patrol.
Jeff Buckley, Kurt Cobain, and Heath Ledger are becoming Jim Morrison, Elvis, and James Dean.
Joachin Phoenix, who became Leaf before re-becoming Joachin, is becoming River Phoenix.
Rufus Wainwright became Judy Garland, but only for one night.
Liza Minnelli is becoming Liberace.

Tony Randall: Debbie Reynolds.
Alec Baldwin wanted to become Marlon Brando but is becoming David Hasselhoff.
Rachael Ray is becoming Tony Danza.
Martha Stewart is becoming Rachael Ray.
Tyra Banks is becoming Farrah Fawcett.
So is George Michael.
Sarah Jessica Parker is becoming Bette Midler, who has become something between the Wayland Flowers puppet Madame and Jean Smart.
Brian Williams is becoming Peter Jennings.
Friendster, MySpace, and Match.com are becoming Facebook, which is becoming Alcoholics Anonymous, choir practice, happy hour, and the new Solitaire.
Manhunt is still Manhunt, though, and that's reassuring.
As is Sean Penn still being Sean Penn, Harry Crews being Harry Crews, and Devotchka still being Devotchka.
Brad Gooch is becoming Gore Vidal—and must have a painting aging in a closet somewhere that is becoming Dorian Gray.
Tim Dlugos is becoming Frank O'Hara.
And what Frank and Tim and Jim became, we are all of them and us becoming.

## COME TO THE DEN OF MY HILLS

Christian moved home and the pipes
of my company house, time to work
the knelt desk, approvingly, expanding
the held mouth and the wanted he opened,
the filling explained, my star-struck
was thrown down and leaned over,
his figured incline thankful its course,
a thankful spent agonizing to feel something
soberly, that sometimes the discount
tanks, the everything hour is full,
                                        and you
can hardly handle another younger
pounded stuttering Christian, motioning
his fine *Almost*, the stretching thing
pressing your breath backwards—
the dragon asana, the rabbit's foot
flinch to Gentile spurts of occupation—
the plowed lessons of pranayama,
twenty-three-year-old salty odorized spectacular:

We were Biblical to be photographed.
He was catching to remember.

## Yellow

Pelican faced boy
Foam shored and sure formed
Ashamed of his father


The drug addict's cigarette
Her contact lens excuse
Her wallpaper monologue


Coward of the county headline
*Bus Stop Bully Hits Big Sis*
*Little Brother Runs*


Dungareed handkerchiefs
Old-fashioned advertisement
Trick to pick pocket


The urine filled fish tank
His pledge class
Proving its brotherhood


On DNA'd sheets
The author signed autographs
*World Famous Love Acts*


Serrano's *Piss Christ*
My organic socks
The Tiffany lampshade

# Quantum Leap

I tried everything, man, shouldered it & didn't
I have to, after graduation when belief turned dark,
a rocky drive of years to say goodnight, I was almost
an island, semi-private & nude, I had the flashlight look

(caught!)  but later I figured those pulled to devotion
were standing in the okay of whispers, calling me to them:
"*You got a ride, denim?*" I wore the loosened powerboat sign
of fingers in belt-loops, lifting the carcass of my dignity.

I found they were there deliberately, protected through pretensions
& I pretended to listen to adoration premeditated but impossible.
The past was an apology. I believed in siestas, I believed minutes
were minutes & considering articulations, indispensable.

## Mistaken Identity

I've been refused entry to a free movie screening because the managing administrator said I was "in the industry." She was convinced I was Ray Liotta.

I've been photographed outside Barney's by Japanese paparazzi who wouldn't believe I wasn't Matt Dillon.

I've been mistaken for Cherokee and apparently I look like everyone in eastern Oklahoma.

When Andre Dubus III was nominated for the National Book Award, a fan shyly approached me with his novel and a pen. I said Andre Dubus III should probably sign it.

One of the Pointer Sisters told me I was a young Mel Gibson. I told her, "I heard he was short."

Tom Hanks, Tony Randall, Robbie Robertson and Robbie Benson.

I remember once in a restaurant, my friend recognized Sandra Bernhard. She stood up at her table and pointed at us, screaming, "Aren't you…?! Aren't you somebody?!"

## Celebrities on Greenwich Avenue

Sam Shepard at Bigelow's.

Minnie Driver at Tea & Sympathy.

Oliver Platt in his pajamas.

The guy from Oz on his motorcycle.

Mary Louise Parker.

Matthew Broderick.

Hillary Swank.

Frank O'Hara (on the Ouija board).

Scott Wolfe with his trainer at Equinox.

Scott Wolfe in the locker-room at Equinox.

Scott Wolfe making eye contact while French kissing his fiancé in the lobby of Equinox.

Mike Myers at Starbucks.

Marie Ponsot speeding out of Integral Yoga.

Cynthia Nixon.

Chad Lowe doing sit-ups at Equinox.

Maggie Gyllenhaal reading in front of Café Bruxelles.

Claire Danes on cell phone waiting for table at Tea & Sympathy.

Sandra Bernhard.

John Cameron Mitchell at Soy Luck Club.

JA at KE's birthday party.

Lady Bunny hailing a taxi.

# L-M-N-ATION

AJ    dead
BL    lives in Kentucky
BA    because crazy was just the beginning
CC    stupid gut
DL    Puerto Rico
EJ    depressed
FD    Christian (but sexy dresser)
GS    Louis Vuitton handbag
HL    no chemistry (him)
IG    was mean to a waiter
JB    small dick
KR    no chemistry (me)
KP    small dick (and married to a woman)
LK    porn star (awesome dick)
the M's    already the M's
NA    NA
OS    too young (no matter how VGL)
PM    dead
QN    fem (great blowjob)
RF    TV star
RX    too much chemistry
SS    a slut
TD    dead (but strongly influencing this poem)
US    Republican
VR, WV, XL    too short, too needy, too fat
??    too cagey
YK    lives in Queens
ZL    doing a show in LA
and my sexy bald neighbor on Jane Street    because
if he hasn't talked to me in five years, he probably won't start tonight

# Cardinal Cross

*(August has a killer middle name)*

You're staring straight into the face of doubt and a spicy chicken sandwich. You overcooked your getting psyched, and it's your saint's day, and you refuse to throw it away, even though you're down $200 from an emergency vet visit, and you're locked in the social insecurity office, where it seems like a lot of people are frequent smokers and occasional bathers. You're too smart to be gritty, not up to touring around with Dr. Feelgood and the Interns exactly, more like in silence therapy, but you're starting to get a vibe from an organ, as if your life were coming true. You wonder if you show your muscle. Your hunger. You see those planets stacking up.

## On the Way to Brotherhood

*(William & Mary)*

your son wrapped up in a columbian hockey
all-nighter    after the game *i never*
*he'd never*    was only joking in the locker-room
his drunk roommate's lips too full   his hair too long
*XXXXXX*          and a perfect excuse
the indian in the closet was hotel block white
in the morning two escapes   three window exits

## 23

    and preening                                  wet right through
    dog-ripe despite                         & feeling it

    how much it feels                      how right
    this morning's peacock stretch    the memory


    as distant as last night              whiff of
    fingers fisted in flex:                 him

                 & in the mirror
                        <u>still you</u>     <u>still whole</u>     <u>still man</u>
                          (23)        (23)          (23)

## Dad Jokes Around before Defining AIDS

He was a mountain gorilla and I was an old lady at the zoo.

There was blood on his clown suit; I was a 15-year-old boy.

He was a light bulb.  I was seven angry lesbians.

Him: the difference between a venereal disease and a sly midget.

Talent scout; Aristocrat.

He: my father.   I: another idiot dick sucker.

## Venus Retrograde

Somebody's back on the lonesome, like a fever
dropped on the city, thinks maybe he will join a fight club
or get a haircut. Somebody back from the breaking
point, shapeshifting, only wanting to be a plant,
preferably a sunflower, somebody dug and somebody
watered. Somebody else is a child. Somebody cannot believe
Exxon Mobil just posted the largest corporate profit in history.
Nothing against Miss America, but the planets,
and for that matter, Earth:   *Hello? Venus? Come back!*

## Holidays in Abu Ghraib

We're looking at 365 days of Halloween
batty black Klansmen

We're looking at angels of death
on a cardboard tree
immortal Christmas

We're electrocuting Easter
sending crucifixion postcards
on the Fourth of July

We're looking at Columbus Day

## Mercury in Uranus

Someone is back from the Gay Pride Parade and oh so proud, and someone is actually sitting in the sun, someone done with her edits, for now, and someone clipping his toenails, someone has fluorescent fingernails, and someone is in San Francisco, someone who can't believe it took him so long to start blogging, don't forget to check it out at www.blogspot.com, and someone is getting home from the hospital, someone back in Wales, and someone is totally kicking Scrabulous ass, someone giving it three and a half stars out of a possible five, two someones independent in Vegas, Viva Las Vegas, and someone with culture clash: from Fleishman's to Dallas, and someone very busy at a two-day conference, someone London, Brighton bound, and someone thinks that cutting the hands off thieves is an appropriate punishment, someone is wondering if the Fourth of July is really an excuse to blow things up, and someone just had a filling fall out, and on a holiday weekend, so no dentists available, and someone is doing voodoo to stop the rain, someone is preparing for flight, someone is all "ding dong Jesse Helms is dead," and someone loves Hydrocodone, someone wonders what message he sent walking down Michigan Avenue with an orchid, someone terrible at the "crying it out" method, and someone thinking through some important issues, someone getting ready to come to New York and someone who just wants to go home, someone is weaving-formatting-weaving-formatting, and someone was halfway to campus before she realized it was Saturday, and she left her bank card in the ATM, and she made two trips to the store and still forgot bird seed, and someone is tired as hell, someone schläft, someone getting ready to go to dinner with his beau, someone is Murder on the Dancefloor…you better not kill the groove, and someone wishes her palm a good Sunday, and someone is in love with her family, and someone hasn't heard from her family in fourteen years.

## NORTHEAST KINGDOM

somewhere you rise knowing fire
razes everything unfired, initiates
the unintended, boils the root-dried
water's scented fall.

once we'd have wakened to snakes
and voles would propagate the pond's
wet lawn. a common blackbird eyes
a red-winged blackbird's empty nest.

and thin slopes of cattails mirror
hemlocks felled, arrowing the day's
direction, further north, shorting summer
its season, its scrawled light.

somewhere your desert ceremony
spans eclipses, girdles the sun
where cedarwood cheats morning
of its thaw. here the dew,
the fog, the dam begin their slide.

# **Yesterday. Toilet. Flush.**

been bit down
the how down

the mind
the gurgling

toilet. thought
that feeling

strange erotic
blurry kind

of blind
the toilet.

the sink
the close bath.

the mean
develops.

successful
afterplay

image.
the toilet.

the climb
the voices

swallowed shock
pulled closer.

the listen
the filling

really
confident.

# If *Nancy* was Aaron Smith

*(after Joe Brainard)*

If *Nancy* was Aaron Smith she'd be close to going to Hell.
She'd be looking for a protégé, pregnant, and terrified
of sex and doctors. She'd be ready for Daniel Craig to examine her,
mother of the first new millennium baby of the whole world.

If *Nancy* was Aaron Smith she'd be doing a bit of damage to us,
and she'd be doing bad damage to herself.
She'd be a human powered vehicle.
She'd be the whore of charm school.

If *Nancy* was Aaron Smith she'd be no stranger to a mixed blessing.
She'd be sick of academic bullshit.
She'd be looking for poems about cock.
She'd be literal.

If *Nancy* was Aaron Smith she'd be a collage of *Our Fathers*
in an Edwin Denby doll house.
She'd be the biggest little state in the union.
She'd be planning a convention.

If *Nancy* was Aaron Smith she'd make cameo appearances
at W.Va. nursing homes and it would take her a while to get back to you.
She'd be about as spiritual as a toaster.
She'd beat the shit out of The Terminator.

## For the Doubts

Kiss a worm before you slip it on a fishhook.
Don't change the name of a ship.
Leave candy on children's graves.
Blow out all the candles on your birthday cake.
Never return a food container empty.
Don't sing at the table.
Throw back the first fish you catch.
Don't chase someone with a broom.
Get out of bed on the same side you get into it.
Carry an acorn in your pocket.
Don't rock an empty rocking chair.
Hide your thumbs during a funeral.
Don't pass food chopstick to chopstick.
Look at the new moon over your right shoulder.
Sleep facing South.
Don't put a hat on the bed.
Don't kill a ladybug.
Don't cut your nails on a Friday.
Place a knife under the bed during childbirth.
Catch a falling leaf on the first day of autumn.
Introduce yourself to empty doorways.
Eat gnocchi on the twenty-ninth of the month.
Kiss under mistletoe.
Don't say goodbye on a bridge.
Don't wear an opal if it isn't your birth stone.
Spit on a new bat.
Don't leave a quilt unfinished.
Plant rosemary by your doorstep.
Don't say Macbeth in a theater.
Don't discuss private matters in front of a cat.
Touch iron when you see a nun.
Don't whistle in the wheelhouse.
Throw coins in the ocean before you sail.
Throw baby teeth on the roof.

Don't point your finger at the moon.
Don't lend or borrow salt.
Don't close a pocketknife unless you opened it.
Tip your hat to a magpie.
Keep your fingers crossed.
Knock on wood.

## FOR TIM (*WHO SAYS HI TO DAVID*)

and your wit on the Ouija
December 11, 2007

*'FUCK OFF A.V.'*
*'GO MAKE LOVE TO PACO'*
You wrote that you watched us
and that you liked it

You said I owed you a poem
I owe you books of poems

You told me *'OPEN THE WINDOW'*
then *'YOU JUST LET IN A GHOST'*

## GOOGLISM FOR: JOE BRAINARD

one of those unclassifiable artists
the best you've never heard of

remembered for his sly pop
among the other artists on the third floor

currently on exhibit at the berkeley art museum
the only poet in the history of the world

# CROW-BLUE, CROW-BLACK

    (ink-voiced)

Crow-Blue, Crow-Black, I have come
to pacify you.

    *(paper-voiced)*

*Ha! Now your body is heavy.*

    (ink-voiced)

I have made your image out of black wood.

    *(paper-voiced)*

*Now you are in a condition to follow*
*the red spider's path in all seven directions.*
*Ha! I have just come to fill you up.*

    (ink-voiced)

Now, crow, with your back turned,
you are ligneous and black.

    *(paper-voiced)*

        *Forgetful*
*of my name and my people. Ha!*
*Now your heart is a dark thicket.*

    (ink-voiced)

I have returned from the stars.
I have returned from the ground.

    *(paper-voiced)*

*I do not need to say Blue.*
*I do not need to say U:ya.*

# CROW-BLACK
*north turns south*

# Thirteen Crow Feathers

In my grandmother's kitchen hang reminders
to my uncles we have to eat what we kill

I have grown up by squirrel   by opossum     and once by canary
an awful tasting story really    so think about venison

We were bird clan      therefore cannibal by religion
talon keychained to our turkey beards

My mother will tell you about dangerous
blue jays      to leave babies alone

A fall is sometimes a jump     sometimes a push
Survival is sometimes rehabilitation

Roost together in groups      Identify your kin
Press against each other       Defend your territory

# How is It?

we stopped for directions to Cabo Polonio
and I smelled *fry bread?* It couldn't be,
I said, telling you quickly my hungry Indian
history.  You replied *Estas son tortas fritas,
una comida del campo desde hace mucho tiempo,*
then *Oh my God, those are my grandfathers!*
And there they were, from Aguas Dulces,
visiting an old friend who ran the roadside stand,
a woman already wrapping the sweet dough
and packing it in a plastic bag with napkins
for us to eat on the sand dunes, trying to figure out
with your grandmother how long it had been
since the last time she'd seen you, only then
as tall as the hand she held at the pocket
of her thin denim skirt, and how was it again
that you and she were related.  I watched this
in English, waiting to taste the difference
I wouldn't find in what your ancestors
and my ancestors fed us.  How is it
we shared this flour and fat they fried
as golden as buttered toast, on a dune buggy
ride to a village without roads or electricity,
ate this ancient bread on ancient rocks
watching seals you call *los lobos
de mar,* envisioning a new Picasso?
We ate these *tortas* as the sun dove,
as the moon rose a day before it would be full,
telling each other the names of our appetites
in two languages winnowed down to basics:
*Do you like me? Do you like the bread? How is it?*

# Mixed-Blood at Catholic School

What was dead here, where water started
pulling strings past thought, past *Don't go
darting where they'll find you?* I asked
about the ruby hair, where mother crossed
someone's lullabies, where she sweetened the stars
against that stripling mirror, filling the cracks
heard down that fisted black river, and her eyes
told who'd won, but only when feelings had closed
over words.  She said my style was in her cocktails,
in her sweaty pulls and shuffled tabs, and this chanting
beside the crowded holding cemetery, wind claiming
it knew where her pockets grabbed consciousness,
was where I might, with indulged restriction,
be made to resemble a living Christ.  I reveled
in jealousy, in cowboys harnessed as heroes,
resurrected in crawfish's magnificent assumptions.
I had venerated ambitions; I had fertile mud
and sterile evergreens; I had questions, claws,
a mettled head.  I had my doubts about the dead
and was swayed from disbelief by the sisters
and their scattered thunder.  I was under water's
leave of reason, left with a crucifix of hunger.

# TO SING A MAN'S LOVE TO YOU

Day One.  Go under water at the glow of morning. Face East. Dry by the sun's rays. Where you hear the beloved whistle, steal his step. Hold his footprints in your hands and whisper, *This is your name. These are your people.*

Day Two.  Wash your face and hands in river water at dawn. Face North. Find the seed of a hardwood tree and hold it in your hands. Speak to it. *This is your name. These are your people.*

Day Three.  Stand in still water at dusk. Wet your hair. Face West. Cup the water in your hands and sing to it. *This is your name. These are your people.* Use this water and the earth imprinted with the love's step to plant the seed in a container that will fit beneath your bed. Let the seed germinate under good dreams.

Day Four.  Rise with the sun and drink four sips of water. Remove the container and raise it in your hands. Face South. Tell it, *This is your name. These are your people.* Replace below your bed.

Repeat this last morning's ritual daily, blessing with water to keep the soil wet, reminding the lover his name, for approximately four weeks or until the seed displays visible roots. Transfer the seed outdoors on a new moon in early sunlight, returning these words in each direction:

*This is your name. These are your people.*

*This is your name. These are your people.*   +   *This is your name. These are your people.*

*This is your name. These are your people.*

## MEDIODÍA

The sun is high above our *pareos,* above
*la playa* where we're reading Idea's

*poemas,* practicing vocabularies and pronunciation.
I read to myself in silence, then to test my tongue

aloud. You understand me, the context
I am quoting, her 65-year-old observations

on the Uruguayan beach at noon. You translate
*"zumba"* — "the drowsy bee's buzz"

then the rest of Vilariño's poem to English, "Is that right?"
We are in communion, we are in love

with the other's language, the ability to speak
across our intonations. On the white

sand behind us, four little girls play *"papa
caliente,"* passing the *fútbol* and counting to *diez.*

In front, an old man pushes a cooler, shouting
*"Helados!"* I tell you it's hot. You get me ice-cream.

## Spider Medicine

I jump the water like an old Indian story
this one has Spider in it too     my son

bitten is good news     he'd turned
14 & wasn't yet pursuing a profession

but his leg swells & the pus grows
so I know he'll be a storyteller if he lives

& he will live because I jump the water
in my johnboat     carry him to his mother

in time     my wife looks at the bite
above his kneecap     the tourniquet I tied

*Red widow* she confirms *Many stories*
she spits on her hands and snaps     *but terrible endings*

## HUNTING SON

Squirrel tail hatbands    coonskin caps    caged descented skunks
Baby beavers in the bathtub    now stuffed
Striking rattlesnake zoo    his dad's taxidermy
His youth "Pet Sematary" sick    scary

Gray fox    mink and jackelope    so life-like in their fur
Bear-headed and buck-antlered the paneled walls stared
Glass-eyed    watching the knife    his hunting vision stabbed
By his father's promise of deer blooding

First kill's required ritual    his hands cutting gutting
Thoughts of all animals' revenge haunt sleep
Death dream    his coffin waits empty    body stolen
Someone's up to something    you know his dad

First he'll have to skin the boy    sew in every hair and
Hug him as he zips him up the back
But in coon skin and camo the boy won't ever cry
And his dad will get the hunting son he wanted

## EXTERIORS

Coffee breast to sweet milk coffee
Bright as the flash in the family photo

Fair-haired mailman's special delivery
Gossiped on the front porch coffee break

*"Where Chebon get them blue blue eyes?"*
Fastest mouse in all of northwest FLA

Hobo dreaming     wolf raised     Tarzan crush
Old man sleeping on the Reeves' back porch

Big sister saved by religion     I slip
Prefer Sunday fishing to church service

Foam ribbons on the blue sea's shore
Dad furious: fish ain't bitin'   *"Quit playin' and piss!"*

Back in boat I'm fly swollen     ivy poisoned     sea sick
Sudden need for quick getaway

Birthday party banter: Betty Jo will run him over
If Mom won't     No, Mom says she can do it

Genetics     heretics     lunatics     deer ticks

Maybe I'll fall in love some day
And have a normal family

## Who's Pretending?

We made syrup from rusty trouble,
a lover's shirt, a road, heat and Okmulgee water,
that flat-footed cloud about to splash whiskey puddles
there where grandfather insisted *Fine*,
cupping into beautiful, where grandmother
found her insulated sugar capsule escape,
where people wore shells like grace —
and minutes later, or hours, eyes furiously pursed,
your *What if* fell asleep, typical
emerging weak like a white scar,
beads lifted like moons, like moments
after a flashforward, another future
soft as the plastic in grandmother's nylons,
when funny was choreographed
toward another *Dear, it isn't you*
morning, manufactured eyes faded,
with enough Indian to wish
water thought water, thought anything
full-blooded as love, as the river –

like that fat, quick-seeded cloud was even interested.

# A Joyful Noise

Rubbing against the music minister after the first day of the Billy Graham crusade in Atlanta, I silently counted the youth group members counting on me to keep the promise made to come back with beer. I always came back with something for the other northwest Florida teens who took a chance on me with their tithing change, our sack of quarters along my front pocket, tan corduroy pants on the floor of the van of the Woodpine Presbyterian Church, my underwear in the hands of the man who directed the choir, now directing me: on my knees, open my throat, watch my teeth, and sing. Later the group would convince me I was the greatest, loading our dormitory bathtub with ice to keep the can beer cold. I was old enough to almost get away with it, but late for the next morning's hymns. And I was strong enough to stand the punishment, 24-hours under the lock and song of our chaperone, which meant sharing his bedroom. I was counting on the two more nights till we got home.

# The Title of the Painting is Saint thomas

saint thomas is happening saint thomas island
saint thomas a child taking part
in all aspects of church life saint thomas
a prime example of all of this saint thomas island
an accredited american sleep academy
a masterpiece of cathedral proportions
saint thomas is being forgotten as saint thomas
saint thomas is consistently called the angelic doctor
saint thomas is a faith

saint thomas is an intimate soup kitchen located in chicago
saint thomas is the highest point saint thomas
saint thomas is often called father of the poor
saint thomas is biblically and fundamentally sound
home to all techniques of animal approach
venerated as the apostle of india
saint thomas is allocated two delegates to the convention
saint thomas is made in the context of the remission of venial sin

saint thomas is december 21 saint thomas
saint thomas is called the universal teacher
saint thomas is here teaching us
saint thomas is looking off into space
saint thomas his symbol saint thomas proverbial
saint thomas is liberum arbitrium
saint thomas is often remembered
for doubting that jesus had been raised from the dead
saint thomas is the title of the painting

## Punta del Este Pantoum

Accept my need and let me call you brother,
Slate blue oyster, wet sand crustacean,
In your hurrying to burrow, wait. Hover.
Parse opening's disaster to creation's

Slate, to another blue-eyed monstrous sand crustacean,
Water-bearer. Hear the ocean behind me,
Pursued, asking to be opened, asking Creation
To heed the tides that uncover you nightly.

Water-bearer, wear the water beside me,
Hide your burying shadow from the shorebirds,
But heed the tides that uncover you nightly.
Gems in sandcastles, stick-written words,

Hidden from the shadows of shorebirds,
Washed over by water. Water's revelatory
Gems, sand, castles, sticks, words—
Assured of erasure, voluntary erosion.

Watched over with warrior resolution,
Crab armor, claws, and nautilus heart,
Assured of a savior, reconstruct your evolution,
Clamor to hear, water scarab, what the tampered heart hears.

A scarab's armor is light enough to fly.
In your hurry to burrow, wait. Hover.
Hear the clamor of the crustacean's heart.
Heed this call of creation. Call me brother.

## St. Nicholas

Once thought the patron saint of shoreham lepers, St. Nicholas made a public apology for being too sexy, that curandero, end-chanting his confession regrettably that he was likely to do it again, meaning *The fox can lose his fur but not his manners*, and that we'd miss his developing affiliation like a mujer guerra. He said *You have to sell it if you want someone to buy it*, and we, the well-known anglers who willingly cohabited with old St. Nick, said *Sell winter?* Imagine the North Pole as the South Pole, a large private garden surrounded by the unusual. Imagine Christmas inserted like church music.

## Anó Grande (You Copyrighted Your Name and Now I Have to Pay You to Say It)

I know you codfish   though you wear a disguise
Not that there is a way or a mood to beat the hot iron

To give the bottle a kiss        to put myself amidst the horses' feet
Like a dog in a neighbor's yard        the son of a cat

Who doesn't kill mice   I still run from cold water
The flesh of the burro is not transparent       the river

Makes noise because there are rocks in it
Another rooster will sing for us

# Good Dog

Intuition reveals the sphere accessible
Immediate formula deciphered says sensible

Curls the bottom of the toothpaste tube
Washes face with Burt's Bees Orange Essence
Listens to Marissa Monte, Babasonicos, Astor Piazzola, Manu Chao
Clips toenails as close as possible
Cleans countertops.
(taking book from bookshelf)
Reads Cortázar

My imaginary dog only barks when I say Speak
We talk of doorways as if they are mothers

## TRUMPET

i took a tablet called angel of the annunciation
i took a tablet called strength of god
i took a tablet called trumpet
in human form & holding a garden

the archangel gabriel was named by god
    he is the angel to call upon
for any matters associated with the moon
a garden holding a human


gabriel the favoured
gabriel commissioned by god
    wings spread
gabriel in the moment         of landing

## Mars Conjunct Venus

Living another day of blissful unemployment,
considering community-based funding,
saying goodbye by the pool in Palermo,
and putting nothing into lazy,
I'm wearing a bathing suit,
writing about the Gemini, revising
the revisions, and feeling nostalgic.
I'm getting into a 2007 state of mind,
playing homemade Ouija with two women
who have questionable morals, dilly-dallying,
deciding not to surrender after all.
I am the smell of curly fries
and the never-ending burning of migration,
starring in a café catastrophe,
trying to untangle the hot Porteño's
French bulldog from the railing.
I'm having a good laugh at the new style,
I'm coming around again.

## BITING ON GINGER

They were delivery men weathered to the sexual narrow of everything,
sitting dreadlocks and bounced brown skin, window thighs and the shower
reward, kneeled to stand like poured honey

Then one afternoon between rolled down and opened, the thick hand
of his stayed fingers and the let believe stone still crouched over,
an ocean of *Don't go now*

And out of the yarn colossus, the nudged balance knocked sorry,
a dangerous catching

The long thought thought greedy: His dungarees.

## St. Solomon and the Reptiles

Wisdom irrigates their thousand shiny scales
and thinking happens, as when the bird broke the glass

with the shamir, shaking Rabbinical literature's unprecedented realm,
the sacred textile loosed above the upper world, the angels

and the terrestrial globe's inhabitants. Solomon knew
what the fish knew, he knew swallowed, and he knew extravagance.

He knew shrinking. The king of demons knew what Solomon knew,
what the fish knew, and stretched between heaven and earth.

He wandered from sea prince to mountain cock, alone,
until the cock dropped the worm, which was brought back

to Solomon. To his key and his table, to his ant-infested valley.

## Misiones

él is talking to his papá,
una mixta de portugues
y español.  i hear him say,
*we are moving to montevideo.*
he says, *punta del este*
*is not like south america at all.*
his father recounts a history
in piriapolis with his mother.
i hear *muy linda, el amor*
*de mi vida.*  when we leave
his father tells me, *visit us*
*again soon.*  this is the way
they say i love you.

with my pa, it's blood
pressure, the doe
my nephew killed,
my latest publication.
he didn't understand it
he says but he liked it.
gabriel nods his head.
*it was about you both,*
i tell them, language barriers.
*en metáforas,* gabriel adds
but dad doesn't think
he speaks that accent.
a few beats later
dad laughs.  *oh metaphors!*
this is the way we say it.

## Postcards for Kenward

I've tattooed *Maria* on the forearms of your photographs.
Today at the flea market an instinct to surprise you.

Antique foreign postcards. A find
among the shoeboxes, 1907 Lesbian Romance!

Dramas! Bold *damas* declare their intentions
to our Lady of Pagola. 103 years ago she lived

on the same street as our rental! Imagine
young Carmen calligraphying *Señorita Catalán*

on the bare skin of the refined elite, re-inking
the hand-painted *postales*. I translate her Spanish

on the back of the decorated damsel, the one
with maroon roses and blue pastel. *"The girlfriends*

*who want you cannot forget you, and to prove*
*my affection I dedicate to you this postcard."*

Kenward, I dedicate to you all I've found today
at the *feria* in 2010 Montevideo, from Avenida Pagola,

where jealous Clara Carrera sent Maria the child
holding her china doll. Rouged cheeks and lips

and Easter Sunday dress. *"They can tell*
*you that they love you,"* she warns our heroine. *"An instant*

*can return itself to the sea. But to love you*
*like I love you... Lies. That can never be."*

I almost wrote on the two blank-backed
cards from the 1930s, but choose to let you

add your own amusing captions to their kitschy drag,
black-browed foreheads white and wide as blank canvas.

*"All is sunny in Uruguay. Wish you were here."* And it is.
And we do. *"Much love to the cats. We'll see you in June."*

# Septipus

*(for the seven-armed Uruguayo)*

1. One to hold the *mate*; to stop a taxi; to extend an index finger to push up loose-eared eyeglasses;
2. One to crook the thermos, pour the water, and redirect cooked yerba with a silver *bombilla*; to light a cigarette;
3. One to puff the *Rojo*; to gesture "*WWWHat a pity!!*"; to act out words our tongues don't know yet;
4. One to fine tune antennae and radiate little summer shocks; to tune the radio to María Rita, *tango electronica,* or The Cranberries;
5. One to good-guard new *amigos* from uneven stones and *otras cosas peligrosas*, bothers and malaria; to offer the growing moon, fireworks;
6. One to scribble a waitress a phone number; to correct a stress from an Italian accent;
7. One of rare perspective to photograph, spell out poetry, convert incantations, cast ordinary objects *artesanal.*

Together these brown arms shoulder the *mochila,* sign shipping orders, protect candles, smudge a room with incense; they envelop children in *abrazos.*

Embrace me also in these seven alchemical arms. Make the *tambores* jealous. Take my hand as we walk along the *rambla* becoming a new metal.

## Man Country

north of Little Rock is famous they told me
the sentence was sold through that that I'd heard
after the printed muscles switched lengthwise

and the horniest straightened
rocked the webbing St. John netted
the map graphing    *What I mean is I'm*

and facing speculation still in his favor
narrowly betting a closing argument pick-up
cloudless semi-private and clean-shaven

gauge stilled and God marking his territory
ushering conditions    conveniences shuttering
the guaranteed hand    my hand

# Snakebird

It is the muskrat's hour at the pond,
a whiskered nose leading an arrowheaded
correspondence, tail under water wagging
like a dog retrieving, and I think about which set
bears easier respect, which necessity is more
properly termed, and when separate beings.
Whereby what character snakes—or mallards,
the male securely perpendicular, a struck chord
on the subended dock; female 100 percent
camouflage. It's hard not to wonder whose regard
rests slightly larger. Whose belly marked.
Whose wrist, whose ankle bound. Crisscross
those crocodiles, those generally extreme
webbed swimming creatures, and the familiar
substance is alteration, is Asclepiades' lodestone,
empiricist style meeting teacher. Facto:
Minute illustration attracts inspection,
until the bats sweep the rippled surfaced method.

## "We Ourselves See in All Rivers"

a knife thrower and a writer
dive la Riviera Maya
grip skulls of neural buoyancy
explain fish luminously blue

Melville almost said *"We see ourselves"*
the briny seasick smell   Matapalo
Quintan Roo in Gran Cenote
the wife of a stranger

a silver moon on Tulum ruins
the temperature of a match
diaphanous     flounderous
like gods ascending

## Inspidered

My nephew is jubilant, his face red. He tells me, "*Tio*, I am inspidered." His eyes grow wide with urgency to speak beyond this new word. Yesterday it was "polka dot," carrying inside the huge palm coconut covered with sand.

Has he been bitten, I worry, remembering the brown recluse who poisoned me, the spider-crab that drowned my sister, but there are no bright bites on his little arms or feet. Beach is falling from his damp, black hair.

"Tell me, *amor*," I say, "How are you *inspidered?*"

"I can swim by myself, *Tio*! The woman under water said I'm never going to drown. Never!"

"*Me alegro, mi vida.* What else did the woman tell you?" I kneel close because I am curious.

"She said I am going to be a champion!"

He has no doubt these are truths. We set aside his tiny life-preserver to give to another child. I tell him I will watch him swim.

"Uncle," he says, "put on your diving suit. You will see I am Champion."

And what would he like to do after swimming, I ask this orphan of the ocean.

"You can hold my hand," he says, "and we can walk down the beach."

"We can pick up polka dots."

# IEMANJA

Today we wear white, carve gourds
to carry our candles and fruits
on the river to the sea. The goddess
hears the waves, the drums
are blessed, and every one of us
is new. Take this silver chain,
this Colorado sage. Bless this
land and all land touched by rain.
Bless women who travel in boats,
men who fish with their hearts, bless
our children. Take this sweet *sandía*
and divide our coins among the thirsty.
May all hungry men eat. May all
men sleep and wake in peace.
May all land be touched with rain.

# Mirror Sonnet

A part of me will always be everywhere
that I've left you     under the streetlamp
on Jane Street     too late to say I'm sorry

Caribbean bound from winter Colorado
outside     unplugged     alone in NYC
and on the Buquebus to Buenos Aires

breaking paralysis by continental shift
climbing a ladder I inked inside my elbow
at The Medicine Show where a fat magician

caught my Intermission Disappearing Act
the subway     tube     numerous taxis
by plane     by canoe     by portage

by the Grand Canyon     both sides
of Yosemite     and from Rome to Nice

you might see me fly back to Rome from Nice
might see my grand plan through both sides

by plain "can do" portage
my own way     to beat numerous exits
during intermission     catch my reappearance at

The Medicine Show where I'm The Magician
climbing the ladder inked inside my elbow
breaking habits of paralysis     real consciousness shit

I'm on the Buquebus from Buenos Aires
(the boat ride after the plane home from NYC)
Montevideo bound I cross the Río

I said goodbye to Jane Street
I left you under the streetlamp
A part of me will always be everywhere

# A Proposal

I am a young man, Fire. You
are a young man, Wood.  Listen,
I will go with you.  In the air,
I enter, ancient. You in the smoke.

Kingfisher just kissed you.
The green frog, he just kissed you.
The dragonfly, wood, water, stone.
Choices are frequently made through inspiration.

A cloth, a chair, a walking stick.
Various symbols to elevate you.
The little white dog made footprints.
You and I just hold up the stars.

# End Notes

**CROW-BLUE**

The first half of this collection, "Crow-Blue," is dedicated to Tim Dlugos and the poet Ai, two writers who've influenced the poet I've become. Ai for daring me to poetry in the first place. Dlugos for sending an emissary whisper to his former apartment, the same one I lived in for ten years in Greenwich Village.

Crow-Blue reflects my experience moving from the southeast to the northeast. Most of these poems were written in New York City and Calais, Vermont.

**POEM$^X$**

I read the mathematical symbols as narrative, where "Poem$^X$" becomes "Poem to the Ex," and equations such as "$x < (y\,x\,y\,x\,y)$" become "ex is less than the sum of why ex why ex why."

**CORVUS & HYDRA**

Based on the one of the myths of the constellations, this summary taken from Wikipedia explains it as:

Apollo sent Crow/Raven (Corvus), who was at the time a white bird, to get water in the god's cup, but Crow waited for some tempting figs to ripen and then had a feast on them. He came back late with a water snake (Hydra) in the cup of water he was sent for. Apollo put Corvus in the sky along with Hydra and the cup. And forever after, in the movement of the constellations, Hydra keeps the water from thirsty Corvus, yet Crow always sees the water, just out of reach.

**TO REMOVE ANGER; CROW-BLUE, CROW BLACK; TO SING A MAN'S LOVE TO YOU**

"Spell poems" imagined from Muskogee, Cherokee, and family remedies.

**POEM TO MY BOYFRIEND'S HUMAN IMMUNODEFICIENCY VIRUS**

    Another spell poem, imagining a weakening of the HIV virus. I lost my first partner, Ash Jordan, to complications from AIDS in 1996. I cast the poem to weaken its power with each incantation, and encourage it to be read aloud. This poem is dedicated to those living with the virus and those living with the memories of loved ones lost.

**SHEDDING**

    Rilke and Satie (named after Rainer Maria Rilke and Erik Satie) were Kenward Elmslie's yellow and white cats that I took care of as the poet's personal assistant in his homes in Vermont and New York. Helvetia Perkins was a friend of Elmslie's and gifted him a green felted wool door covering to cast protection on his bedroom in Calais, Vermont.

**GREENWICH AVENUE**

    Studying with poet/professor Lisa Jarnot in my MFA program at Brooklyn College, she asked me if I'd read much of Tim Dlugos, as she saw similarities in his work and new poems I was writing. I didn't know of him, so she brought me a copy of his collection *Powerless*. I was floored by the passion, directness, and humor in his poems. And I saw the similarity in the spacing and subjects of some of the lines I'd begun using.

    I became obsessed with Dlugos. I searched for everything I could find about him, his work and his life. I felt a kinship to Tim's writing and literally felt Tim's presence around me, like he was whispering over my shoulder.

    A few days later, I sat down for breakfast with my boss, Kenward Elmslie, and told him: "Kenward, I have become an absolute fanatic of this poet my professor told me about. I feel like his ghost is following me around and talking to me. I want to read everything he wrote and I want to know everything about him. I wonder if you knew him. His name was Tim Dlugos."

Kenward hooted and then looked at me seriously. He said, "That makes sense. Tim used to live in your bedroom."

I am incredibly grateful for the editorial work of David Trinidad in keeping Tim's poetry in print, including editing the recent collection of Dlugos's complete poems, *A Fast Life* published by Nightboat Books.

**EVOLUTION**
Imitation of Tim Dlugos's poem "*Turning*."

**MISTAKEN IDENTITY**
True story.

**L-M-N-ATION** and **CELEBRITIES ON GREENWICH AVENUE**
Dlugos imitations.

**CARDINAL CROSS, VENUS RETROGRADE, MERCURY IN URANUS, MARS CONJUNCT VENUS**
Informal astrological studies of friends' Facebook statuses on the day the titled celestial events formed in the skies.

**ON THE WAY TO BROTHERHOOD** and **23**
Inspired by the haunting and erotic paintings of New York artist Geoff Chadsey, who I also thank for loaning me his copy of "*Jesus' Son*."

**IF *NANCY* WAS AARON SMITH**
Inspired by poet/artist Joe Brainard's reinterpretations of the Ernie Bushmiller comic strip character *Nancy*. Written for Aaron Smith.

**CROW-BLUE, CROW-BLACK**
In the way I understand it, *U:ya* is an underworld Cherokee deity whose name can only be spoken by the dead.

## CROW-BLACK

The second half of this collection, "Crow-Black," is dedicated to my partner, Gabriel Padilha, and to my best friend, Gabriel Insiburo.

Crow-Black reflects my returns home to the Florida/Alabama border, and my experience as a North American living in South America. These poems were written in Molino, Florida; Montevideo, Uruguay; and Misiones, Argentina.

### THIRTEEN CROW FEATHERS

Direct descendants of Richard L. Taylor (*Hadjo Pokke*) and Susannah Hosford (*Jo-jo-lon-fab*) from Poarch and Eufala, Alabama, through my mother's family we are Bird Clan (*Fuswalgi*) of the Poarch Band of Muskogee Creek Indians. The Poarch Band is made up of thirteen original Creek families who hid in the Escambia County, Alabama, swamps to avoid Andrew Jackson's Trail of Tears. My heritage also comprises Scottish, French-Canadian, Micmac, and Mallorcan ancestry.

### HOW IS IT

Cabo Polonio and Aguas Dulces are coastal towns in eastern Uruguay, where I was astonished to smell and taste Fry Bread, a traditional American Indian food, on my first visit to South America.

"*Estas son tortas fritas, // una comida del campo desde hace mucho tiempo*" = "These are fried cakes // an old-time bread from the countryside."

"*los lobos // de mar*" = "the sea wolves" (also known as sea lions).

### MEDIODÍA

Idea Vilariño is another poet whose work and life have become an influence. Vilariño was a Uruguayan poet, 1920-2009, and part of the group of poets known as *Generación del 45*. She is the author of volumes including *La Suplicante, Poemas de Amor* and *No*.

*mediodía* = noon
*pareos* = sarongs
*la playa* = the beach
*zumba* = buzz
*papa caliente* = hot potato
*fútbol* = soccer ball
*diez* = ten
*Helados* = ice cream

### PUNTA DEL ESTE PANTOUM

Punta del Este is a beach/resort city on the eastern shore of Uruguay.

A pantoum, as defined by Wikipedia, is a form of poetry similar to a villanelle in that there are repeating lines throughout the poem. It is composed of a series of quatrains; the second and fourth lines of each stanza are repeated as the first and third lines of the next. This pattern continues for any number of stanzas, except for the final stanza, which differs in the repeating pattern.

### ANÓ GRANDE

A remarkable bird I encountered in northern Argentina. It is also known as the Greater Ani, or the Black Cuckoo. To me it looks like a big blue Crow or Raven. I saw one first at Güira Oga, a bird refuge (literally Bird House in the indigenous Guaraní language) near Iguazu Falls.

### MISIONES

My partner Gabriel's mother is Uruguayan; his father is Brazilian. The Padilhas raised Gabriel and his siblings in Misiones, Argentina.

Piriapolis is a city on the eastern coast of Uruguay.

*"muy linda, el amor // de mi vida."* = "very pretty, the love // of my life."

### POSTCARDS FOR KENWARD

My dear friend and former boss, poet Kenward

Elmslie, collects postcards and I found for him some old ones at the *fería* in Montevideo. Two of them had been written on by a lesbian in 1907 writing to her lover at an address on the same street where Gabriel and I were renting a house. Kenward had previously written a poem as a gift for me, "Head Dance," in which he incorporated postcard images into the verse. I attempt the same kind of tribute to Kenward in this poem. It is dedicated to him.

"*damas*" = ladies

Calle Pagola is the street in Pocitos neighborhood of Montevideo where we lived in 2009 and to where the postcard had been originally addressed.

*postales* = postcards
*fería* = street market

### Septipus

Uruguayans seem to be able to do a lot of things at one time. Even with their arms full, they seem to grow another one to lend a hand. Written for Gabriel Insiburo.

*mate* = cup for drinking *yerba mate*, the tea everyone in Uruguay is crazy about, like North Americans and their Starbucks

*yerba* = the tea leaves
*bombilla* = the metal straw they drink mate out of
*Rojo* = Marlboro Red
*tango electronica* = electronic tango
*amigos* = friends
*otras cosas peligrosas* = other dangerous things
*artesanal* = artistic
*mochila* = backpack
*abrazos* = hugs
*tambores* = drums
*rambla* = long sidewalk that lines the Montevideo coast

### Inspidered

*Tío* = uncle
*amor* = love, here used as term of affection

*Me alegro, mi vida*—I'm happy, my life (my life used as term of affection)

## IEMANJA

Iemanja is the Umbanda goddess of the ocean. She is celebrated throughout the world, with holy days designated in Africa, Brazil, Cuba, Haiti, and Uruguay. In Montevideo, the city's residents gather on February 2 at Playa Ramirez to offer the goddess gifts and ask for blessings for the coming year.

s*andía* = watermelon

## A PROPOSAL

Written for Gabriel Padilha.

The New York Quarterly Foundation, Inc.
New York, New York

## Poetry Magazine

**Since 1969**

Edgy, fresh, groundbreaking, eclectic—voices from all walks of life.

Definitely NOT your mama's poetry magazine!

The *New York Quarterly* has been defining the term contemporary American poetry since its first craft interview with W. H. Auden.

*Interviews • Essays • and of course, lots of poems.*

**www.nyquarterly.org**

No contest! That's correct, NYQ Books are NO CONTEST to other small presses because we do not support ourselves through contests. Our books are carefully selected by invitation only, so you know that NYQ Books are produced with the same editorial integrity as the magazine that has brought you the most eclectic contemporary American poetry since 1969.

## Books

**nyqbooks.org**

poetry at the edge™

## About the Author

Chip Livingston is the author of a previous poetry collection, *MUSEUM OF FALSE STARTS*, and a chapbook, *ALARUM*. Individual poems, short stories, and essays have been published in journals including *Ploughshares, The Potomac Review, Mississippi Review, Court Green,* and *New American Writing*. His work has been included in the anthologies *SING: Poetry of the Indigenous Americas, SOVEREIGN EROTICS, BEST NEW POETS 2005, BEST GAY POETRY 2008*, and on the Poetry Foundation's website. He has received awards from Native Writers' Circle of the Americas, Wordcraft Circle of Native Writers and Storytellers, and the AABB Foundation. Chip has taught writing and literature at University of Colorado, University of the Virgin Islands, Brooklyn College, and Gotham Writers Workshops. He grew up in the Florida panhandle, spent a decade in Manhattan, and now lives in Montevideo, Uruguay.

www.ingramcontent.com/pod-product-compliance
Lightning Source LLC
LaVergne TN
LVHW041342080426
835512LV00006B/587